LAST NIGHT ANOTHER SOLDIER

LAST NIGHT ANOTHER SOLDIER

Andy McNab

BBC
LARGE
PRINT

First published in 2010 by
Transworld Publishers
This Large Print edition published
2010 by BBC Audiobooks by
arrangement with
Transworld Publishers

ISBN 978 1 4056 2285 1

This novel is based on the play *Last
Night Another Soldier*, broadcast by
BBC Radio 4 in August 2009

British Library Cataloguing in Publication Data available

**Advice: contains strong
language and violent scenes.**

Printed and bound in Great Britain by
CPI Antony Rowe, Chippenham and Eastbourne

Chapter One

It was going to be another long night. The Taliban weren't giving up those poppy fields as easily as we had first thought. We were now eight years on from when the British Army first rolled into Afghanistan, and we were still aggressive camping, that's what we call fighting, on both sides of the Helmand River. The whole area was known as the 'Green Zone'. Basically, hundreds of miles of green fields where the local lads grew maize and poppies.

Sergeant MacKenzie told us that Afghanistan supplied ninety per cent of the world's heroin and made the Taliban shedloads of money. He said it was up to us to stop it. Clear. Hold and Build was what the Americans wanted us to do. Kick the Taliban out of the area, take control, and then maybe the farmers wouldn't

1

have to grow poppies for the Taliban no more. Good plan, but the thing is MacKenzie forgot to tell the Taliban. They just kept on coming out of the maize, shooting at us like they never wanted to stop.

That night was my first ever fire fight, and we'd already been hard at it for over four hours. Up until then, I'd only ever practised being a soldier back in the Army Training Centre in Catterick. I'd never actually done it for real.

I was eighteen and had only been in Afghanistan for three weeks. And there I was, stuck behind a mud wall for cover, in a major contact with the Taliban. Not that I'd actually seen the enemy yet. It was so dark out there in the fields, and the maize was so thick, that all I could see was the flash of their weapons pointing towards me when they shot at us. What made it worse was that the flashes seemed to be getting brighter and brighter, which could only mean the Tali were getting closer and closer.

Out of nowhere, a lightning flash from one of their rocket-propelled grenades streaked across the sky. It headed straight towards us. Some of the lads yelled out, 'RPG!' but none of us needed the warning; we were already taking cover. After a rocket flash, there was always a couple of seconds of nothing, then boom . . . you never knew where it was going to hit. Or whether, that time around, it was going to be you.

I got lucky. The rocket hit some rocks about ten metres away from where I was crouched down. I waited a couple of seconds, then got the weapon back onto my shoulder, ready to fire again. Out of the corner of my eye, I saw Toki do the same. Even though he was only a couple of metres away, he needed to yell above the sound of the Apache attack helicopters overhead.

'Briggsy, they're closing in on the

left. They're nearly on top of us. Move up on the parapet. Go!'

I did what I was told. Toki was my corporal, and when he told you to do something, you did it. He was a big giant of a man from Fiji. Cool, calm, with the world's flattest nose and hands like shovels. He'd joined the army to make his fortune, he told us. That was a laugh. He'd be hard-pushed on what they paid us. But I was glad he was my boss. I liked him. Even though he was in charge of our patrol, it still felt like he was one of us.

I ran up to the top of the parapet to join Si and Flash. I could hear the Taliban hollering and shouting at us from the other side of the mud wall. They were obviously closing in, but I still couldn't see a thing out there.

Si gobbed in the mud before he spoke, 'Mate, where are they? I can't see a thing!'

I caught a glimpse of three dark shapes moving left to right across the open ground. 'There. Look! Half left.' I started to fire, then Si and Flash joined in. The Tali were getting a bit too close for comfort, but I still wasn't scared. I had a big, fat SA80 rifle in my hands, plus I had new mates.

Si was one of them. He had white blond hair and a face full of zits that he couldn't stop squeezing. His crew-cut made him look harder than he actually was. He was only a year older than me and was already married to some Polish bird. He came from Liverpool or somewhere like that. He must have done as he sounded just like the curly-haired scouse geezer in *Hollyoaks*.

'Mate, you're right. They're heading for our bit of wall by the looks of it.' His voice rose higher as he realized quite how close they'd got.

Flash reloaded his weapon with a fresh thirty-round mag without looking down. We all needed to stay focused on the darkness for any sign of movement. 'Keep switched on, Briggsy. They're trying to take one of us alive. They've been trying for weeks now . . . let's make sure we don't let them.'

There was a muzzle flash about twenty metres in front of us. We all gave it a five-round burst. The Taliban didn't fire back. All the same, all three of us kept on firing into the darkness to make sure they never would.

Flash was another mate in my patrol. He was called Flash only because he wasn't. He was much older than the rest of us, even older than my mum, I think, but he was sound. His hair was totally grey and he had a chin big enough to balance a mug of tea on. All he needed was a dance partner and he'd be Bruce Forsyth's long-lost twin brother.

Flash was in the Territorial Army, so of course all the patrol gave him a hard time for being a part-time soldier. Even I, the new boy, was allowed to join in. He came from way up north, near some big car factory. They'd made him redundant and then he'd lost his house. So with a wife and two boys older than me, he was out here aggressive camping with us lot just to pay the bills.

Flash glanced down at the mags in his chest harness and jerked his head round to the right. 'They're getting closer. Toki, we need more ammo. More ammo!'

Toki's voice boomed over to us above the sound of gunfire, 'Stand your ground! John's coming with the ammo. He's coming!'

I looked over my shoulder and could just make out John's massive body as he staggered through the mud, his boots sinking deeper with every step. He was trying to run but was almost doubled over with the weight of the ammo boxes. John was a good laugh. He was from Peckham like me, only from a different estate.

More muzzle flashes kicked off in the darkness as the Talis tried to shoot at us. I raised my rifle back over the wall, aimed at the burst of light and pulled the trigger. Nothing happened.

'Stoppage!'

I needed to let everyone know I couldn't fire before I took cover and sorted out what had happened. I landed on my arse, cocked the weapon and tried to get my finger in to free up whatever was stuck in there. The hot metal of the working parts burnt my fingers, but I kept on digging. Rounds were slamming into the other side of our wall as the Talis kicked off again.

There was a piercing scream and a dull thud as a body fell into the mud behind me. I already knew who'd been hit before I spun round.

'Man down, man down,' I yelled into the air. It was John.

He screamed out in the darkness, his arms and legs jerking about in the mud as he fought the pain. Toki's voice came over as calm as ever, taking control of the situation. 'Get that weapon going, Briggsy! Cover us. Flash, with me. Get John.'

Flash broke into a run, bending down low for cover as more rounds slammed into the wall, while Si returned fire from just above me. My fingers kept fumbling with the empty case that was blocking the weapon. I told myself to slow down and stay calm, but it wasn't working. All I could hear or think about was the sound of John screaming. I knew the screaming was good. So long as he was screaming, he was breathing, and that meant he was still winning!

Toki was on the radio, calling in MERT, the Medical Emergency Response Team. I willed the Chinook to come quickly, lift John out and get him to hospital in Camp Bastion.

The screaming started to die down a bit. Flash must have pumped some morphine into John after plugging up any holes and getting more fluids in to replace lost blood. I could hear Toki clearly as he gave MERT a sit rep (situation report).

'Confirm. We have a T1 casualty, Tango 1. We need MERT now.'

That wasn't good. T1 meant we were losing him. He was critical. Flash was thinking the same as me. 'Where the hell is that Chinook!'

I got the empty case out of the weapon and was back in action.

'It's clear, Si!'

'I'll get the ammo. We need more ammo!' Si ran over to where John lay screaming and jerking about as if he was getting electric shocks. I scrambled onto my knees just as a three-round burst of Taliban fire hit the wall. I leant my chest into the mud bricks and got the weapon back into my shoulder. I never got to take aim, though. My rifle jolted skywards and a dark mass rose up from the other side of the wall.

Two large hands glued themselves to the front of my weapon. I tried to pull back but lost my footing, and a Tali the size of a house started to climb over the wall. He was using my rifle to help lever himself over.

As his feet inched higher up the wall, he pulled the barrel down hard onto his shoulder, the hot steel singeing the cloth of his shirt. He took no notice as the heat burnt through to his skin. The stench of sweat, cigarettes and burning flesh hit my nostrils, and within seconds the giant hands flailed out again, this time grabbing hold of my chest harness.

I scrambled backwards to escape his grasp, but he was quicker and stronger. He pulled me back towards the wall, trying to force me over with him. My helmet crashed into his head as I tried to headbutt him, but he took the pain and kept on pulling. I don't know what I shouted, but I yelled and screamed into his face as I butted him again, using all my body weight to stay on the right side of the wall. We were so close I could feel his beard scratch against my face. His spit sprayed into my eyes as he screamed back at me, his eyes fixed on mine.

I clung to the butt of my weapon as I tried to heave back against the pull on my chest harness. Getting rounds off was my only chance. I tried to curl my finger around the trigger, but couldn't make it. He pulled down heavily again, and my feet left the ground. My body inched forward over the top of the wall. I arched my spine backwards, resisting with everything I had, but it was no good. I was hooked like a fish.

I heard Toki shout something again and again. His voice grew louder as he ran towards me, but still I couldn't make it out. He kept on yelling and then finally it sunk in. 'Pistol, Briggsy. Pistol!'

I'd forgotten I had one in my thigh

holster. I let go of my weapon with my right hand and the Tali felt the change in pressure. He leant back once more, putting all his weight into toppling me forward. I felt my hip bones pressing into the ridge. I could hear myself breathing loudly as I pushed my hand down my leg, feeling for the pistol grip.

My fingers closed around the hard steel and I pulled the weapon out of its holster. I raised my arm, brought the pistol round in front of me and shoved it in the Tali's face. As soon as the barrel made contact with skin and bone, I squeezed the trigger hard. One shot straight to the head. His giant hands let go of me and his body dropped like a stone, crashing into the darkness on the other side of the wall.

I pushed myself off the wall just as Toki reached it. He grabbed hold of my body harness and half dragged me over to where Flash and Si were crouched down beside John. I didn't know if I was looking for praise or comfort from my two mates, but I could tell by their bowed heads and motionless bodies that the two of them had other things on their mind. John was no longer screaming . . . or breathing.

Chapter Two

It was just after seven o'clock when we got back to the Forward Operating Base (FOB). There was no time for breakfast, we were straight back to our patrol's eight-man tent to clear away John's kit. You'd think you might get a bit of time off to take it all in, but maybe that was the point. Best just get on with things and not think too much about anything.

The four of us sat around John's bed space. Or at least the other three sat. I stayed standing as my arse was killing me. We were all going through John's kit, stuffing his gear into bin liners so it could be shipped home to his wife.

Si had switched on John's radio while we worked. I reckoned we were all glad of that as it saved us having to say anything to each other.

Well, there wasn't really much to say. When the news came on at half past, we all stopped to hear the report on Afghanistan. As usual, the news girl kept it brief:

'Last night in Afghanistan, British Forces continued their military offensive against the Taliban. Over three thousand British troops are currently taking part in Operation Condor. Their aim is to take control of the Taliban poppy-growing region in Southern Afghanistan. The MoD's spokesperson, Major Jennifer Dufton, said that British ground forces were encountering small pockets of resistance, but that good progress was being made . . .'

Si got really pissed off and hit the Off button. 'Good progress my arse. I can't listen to any more of that crap.' He leant forward on the bed and pulled out John's patrol pack from underneath it. Toki nodded his agreement, and pointed at a pile of thin blue airmail letters sticking out of the top.

'Flash. Those blueys. Sit down and read 'em. Check they're all from John's wife, will you? Or his mum and dad. If not, burn them.'

Flash shook his head as he bent down for the blueys. 'The man's dead. It's not right.'

'I know, but do you really want his wife reading letters from some other woman? They could just be from a sister, but we can't take that chance, mate. It happened in Basra when a guy from A Company got hit by a sniper. His wife got all his personal kit, and in there was a pile of blueys from another woman. John's family have enough problems as it is.' Toki scanned our faces as if searching for clues. 'That goes for all of us. Let's get John's stuff sterile. If we see anything dodgy, bin it.' Flash quickly started sorting through the blueys while we got back to sorting out John's kit.

I kicked a pile of magazines with my boot. 'What about these, Toki? *FHM, Zoo . . .*'

'Cookhouse. Julie won't want those. Anyone know if he has any porn on his laptop?'

I started to pick up the magazines. 'I know he was making a music video using all the film he'd been taking.'

'I'll check it out while you lot are on fatigues. Don't want Julie seeing us chewing up Taliban either.'

Red flecks appeared on Si's cheeks joining his zits like some crazy dot-to-dot quiz. His eyes flashed between us. 'He's dead, and for what? For nothing, that's what. Three days aggressive camping just to get a good kicking? We should have stayed and smashed 'em up big time.' He brought his fist down hard on the bed. 'At least John would have died for something. Where are the pencil necks giving these orders? I didn't see any of them out there last night.'

He was right. No one from HQ ever came to our FOB. I started rolling up John's sleeping bag. 'Probably sitting in those air-conditioned Portakabins in Kandahar, never even been in the Green Zone. Why did they rip us out, Toki?'

Toki was checking out the rest of the patrol pack, pulling out dirty socks and dark-green sweat-stained T-shirts. 'D Company were getting hit big time last night. They needed all the Apaches and support up north. Once they've cleared and are holding their area, we'll be going out on the ground again.'

I put the pile of magazines on top of three bags of boiled sweets, which were all destined for the cookhouse. 'Better had! Makes us look like right wimps.'

Si wasn't finished yet. 'Why ain't we

got loads of helis and all the gear like the Yanks got?'

Toki sighed, raising his legs and plonking his desert boots on John's camp bed. 'No money, I guess. Never is.' We all nodded as we knew it was the truth.

A calm female voice came over FOB's loud speaker system. 'Standby. Standby. Firing. End of message.' Sure enough, the rattle and whoosh of two massive rockets kicked off into the sky. We called them 70km Snipers, because they could still reach their targets from that far away. At least this time it was our guys giving the Talis the good news.

Toki shoved everything he'd been sorting through back into John's patrol kit. There was nothing to be found. 'D Company must still be getting a hammering,' he said.

Toki wasn't wrong. D company were getting smashed up big time on the other side of the valley. It was taking all our helis to keep the Talis down. Another rocket kicked off, forcing Si to shout above it as he picked at a new zit on the side of his neck. 'Hey, Briggsy, heard you did a touch of the old Kung Fu Panda with a Tali this morning, right before you head-jobbed him. Good one, mate.'

'Yeah. Sort of.' I wasn't sure if I wanted to talk about it, so I stared into the bin liner I'd just put John's iPod into, in the hope that we could just carry on packing the kit away.

'And?' Si wasn't going to let it go that easily. 'Mate, what happened? Cough up.'

'Well . . .' I revved myself up to tell the story as best I could.

Si nodded with excitement as I explained what had happened. I tried to tell it as dramatically as I could, because I knew that was what he wanted to hear. 'All I could hear was Toki yelling, "Pistol. Pistol." I was flapping so much I'd forgotten about it. So I reached down to my leg holster and jammed my pistol into his nut and slotted him. Job done. Cheers, Toki.'

'No biggy. I'd have done it for you if I'd been able to get near enough. You were too close to him for me to be able to fire from that far away. Anyway, you did well. Have a dig about for his laptop lead, will you, Briggsy? It might be in with all that stuff in your bin liner.'

I dug around in my sack and pulled out the only lead that looked as if it might work. Si kept looking in my direction, waiting for more of my story. When he realized that was it, he gave me a big thumbs up with both hands.

'Good one, mate. Like you said, job done. Big time!' He beamed at the three of us like he was over the moon I'd killed someone, but maybe he was just pleased that he'd finally burst his zit.

I hoped that would be the end of the conversation, but I should have known he wouldn't leave it there. 'Mate, just think what would've happened if they had, you know, got you? We'd be watching you online getting your head cut off.' Si slid his index finger across his throat. 'Cos you know they'll get one of us one day, don't you? They keep trying. I just hope it ain't me.'

It went quiet for a bit as we all thought about what would happen if one of us got taken by the Talis.

'Hey, Briggsy.' Si still wasn't done. 'You think they'll, you know, give you one before cutting you up?'

Flash lowered the bluey he'd been opening and rolled his eyes. 'You've been watching too much TV, mate.'

Then I remembered something I'd seen on Dave TV about Afghanistan. 'I watched a thing about them playing rugby, but on horses using human heads instead of balls.'

Flash pointed the bluey at me like a school teacher with a ruler. 'It's called buzkashi and it's a game like polo. They usually use a dead goat instead of a ball, but they decided to use Russian squaddies' heads when they were at war with them back in the eighties.'

Si gave a low whistle. 'See, Briggsy, you're lucky.'

I thought Toki would shut them all up at this point. It wasn't really something I wanted to think about. But Toki stopped what he was doing and looked towards the tent flap as if he was going to tell us something he didn't want anyone else to hear.

'They won't stop until they do get one of us alive. If I get cornered, I'm going down fighting. No way are my parents going to see me ripped apart on a computer screen.'

We all looked at the tent flap, too, mostly because we didn't know what to say to that. As usual, it was Si who broke the silence. 'Hey, Briggsy, you gotta keep that as living history.' He jabbed a nicotine-stained finger in my direction. I hadn't a clue what he was on about.

He pointed again. 'Mate, your shirt. You're covered in Tali blood. You got to keep it as a memento.'

I looked down, dropping my bin liner and spilling its contents all over the plastic floorboards that kept out the dust. The right sleeve of my shirt was stained a sticky brown where the Tali's blood had soaked into it. I tugged at my cuff to get it away from my arm, to get the man off me. I don't know how I hadn't noticed it before. I felt sick.

'Jesus!'

I started to rip the thing off my back when Sergeant MacKenzie stuck his head through the flap.

'No, not Jesus. Sergeant MacKenzie to you. But I like your thinking, Briggsy.'

All I wanted to do was get into the shower and scrub the blood off, but I knew there were no showers until just before evening scoff that night. So I was stuck with it. 'Yes,

Sergeant.'

I saw MacKenzie look down at my shirt, so I tried a pathetic joke to make myself feel better. 'Better his blood than mine, eh, Sergeant?'

Sergeant MacKenzie didn't miss a beat. 'I'd say there's still some debate on that . . . Right, listen in, you lot.' He looked at each one of us in turn. 'I want the whole platoon in the cookhouse now. Corporal Tokibaku, get this lot moving.' He turned on his heel and was gone.

Flash gathered up John's stash of blueys. 'You got a cynical mind, Toki. They're all from Julie, right enough. Well, aside from the stack from Jennifer Aniston and Angelina Jolie, of course . . .'

Flash gently returned them to John's kit bag. He didn't want them all crumpled up for John's wife, who would probably keep them for ever. 'I never met Julie or the kids, but me and John were going to get our wives together after this. You know on holiday.' He looked close to tears and could hardly get the destination out without his voice breaking. 'Tenerife.'

The rest of us looked down, pretending we hadn't noticed, and I got real busy with the bin liner. But the truth is we all felt the same. Flash knew it and made a half-hearted attempt to lighten the mood. 'Si, throw those combats over.'

Flash held them up for all of us to see. 'Look at the size of that waist. No wonder it was tough carrying all that lard onto the MERT heli, eh? Bet those doctors thought they'd never get airborne again!'

We all sniggered but it didn't last long and we soon fell silent again. It was hot in the tent now as the sun was higher. Toki shoved the patrol pack back under John's bed. 'Come on, everyone. Let's go!'

Chapter Three

We made our way though the four-inch-thick dust towards the cookhouse. I had to half close my eyes against the bright sun because, as usual, I'd left my sunglasses back in the tent.

We knew exactly why MacKenzie wanted all of us in the cookhouse. By the time we got there, the long trestle tables had already been pushed to one side, and the whole FOB—about seventy scruffy, sweaty soldiers—were standing around waiting for it to start. Toki grabbed four warm beers from the back of the room and handed one to each of us. Like everyone else, we didn't open them, we just stood there holding a can in one hand.

Sergeant MacKenzie stepped forward to face us. His tanned face matched the colour of his totally bald head. He came straight to the point.

'Right, listen in. Rifleman John Hammond is dead. But you lot are still alive. Look around you. Go on, look at each other.'

I looked at Si who stared me out, daring me to blink before he did. I stared straight back at him as MacKenzie continued. 'Remember what we were told before we came out here. One in ten of us is going to be a casualty. So if we don't stay switched on and keep our minds in gear, the next casualty could be the very lad you're looking at now.'

I blinked on purpose and looked away. I wasn't in the mood for Si's stupid games.

Sergeant MacKenzie moved his head about, making eye contact with as many of us as he could. 'It's our job to look out for each other. And to remember John, your mate. Remember all of those who've died, because none of those pencil necks in the real world will. This time next year they'll still be wetting themselves over Beckham's new haircut, Jordan's latest tit job and Jamie Oliver reinventing toast. No point being angry about it, that's just the way it is. Even Iraq is a distant memory for them. It's up to you to keep our guys' memories alive. Because they are one of us. They are soldiers, just like you.'

MacKenzie pulled the ring tab back on the beer can he was holding in his left hand. I knew what was coming, but it felt worse this time around. All of us pulled our tabs back and the room let out a long hiss. Everyone's eyes were on MacKenzie. 'To keep John's memory alive, you've got to stay alive, so keep switched on and look out for each other. It's your job.' MacKenzie raised his arm high in a toast. 'To Rifleman John Hammond. To John.'

We lifted our cans in response and toasted our dead mate. It all felt a bit overdramatic, a bit unreal, but we had to do something for John. Sergeant MacKenzie gave pretty much the same toast every time we lost a lad. This was number sixteen and the battalion was still only halfway through its tour. Good job we weren't doing it for the wounded, too, or we'd be out of beer by now. Not that it was real beer, of course. Alcohol-free Heineken was all we were allowed.

Chapter Four

As I left the cookhouse, Sergeant MacKenzie screamed over to me. 'Briggsy! Stand still.'

I did as I was ordered. Got my feet together, arms down by my sides, and waited.

'Yes, Sergeant?'

Everyone was scared of MacKenzie. Stupid really. He sounded harsh, but the man was a star. It was his job to control us. He had to keep us together, to stop anyone falling apart over John, or anyone else getting zapped. Or worse than that, getting bits of them blown off.

To MacKenzie we were all dickheads, but the thing is, we were his dickheads. He always stuck up for us, even when we'd cocked something up. Last week he punched another sergeant from HQ Company for picking on one of the platoon. That's the sort of dad I would have liked. At least in MacKenzie I had one while I was there.

He hovered over me, pointing a stubby finger at me. 'What's wrong with you?'

'I think I got cut up a bit last night, Sergeant.' I tried to be all casual about it. If Toki was right and everyone was going back into the Green Zone soon, I wanted to make sure I was going with them.

'You seen the medic?'

I shrugged. 'No, Sergeant. It's no big—'

'Wind your neck in,' he bellowed. 'Who do you think you are? Schwarzenegger, the Terminator?'

'No, Sergeant.'

'Correct. So get hobbling over to the medic centre. Get Corporal Rankin to sort it now.'

'Yes, Sergeant.'

Chapter Five

As I lay on the bench in the Medical Centre, I realized I was in a pretty ridiculous position. I was lying on my stomach with my combats around my ankles and my bare arse facing the ceiling. The tinny sound of the Red Hot Chili Peppers rang out from Emma's cheap iPod speakers. Emma was pretty. She was Scottish, with long dark hair that she pulled back in a ponytail. As she leant over the bench to examine me, I prayed my arse wasn't covered in zits.

Emma's voice was kind but matter-of-fact. 'Right then, Briggsy. What did you do, exactly?'

I stared down at the plastic flooring. 'Don't know. Must have cut my arse during the contact last night.'

She put one hand on the edge of the bench and the other on the back of my thigh as she leant in closer. Her movement made me flinch in pain so I thought I'd try to chat a bit to distract myself. 'Emma, d'you really like the Chili Peppers?'

'I'd rather have one of them lying half naked in front of me than you.' She smiled and prodded carefully, but not carefully enough.

I let out a yelp. 'Whoah. That's it, right there.'

She burst into laughter. 'Stop being a wimp, Briggsy.' She prodded again.

'Ow!'

She kept on with her examination. 'Keep still, get a grip . . . that's no cut. I think we can safely say, David Briggs, you have been well and truly shot in the arse.'

My heart sank. Not that it came as a great surprise really. I hadn't been able to sit down all morning because of the pain. I'd hoped it was just a cut, and the news that it was something worse got me flapping. I twisted round to look at her. 'There a bullet in there?'

She shook her head. 'No, it just nicked you. Here, have a look in the mirror. I'll hold it up for you. See how it just went in and out in less than, what, a centimetre?'

I twisted my body round some more. There was a gash in my arse, but the fact that there was no bullet to dig out was a big relief. I started to worry about something else. 'Don't tell anyone, will you, Emma? It's not exactly macho is it? I'll get a hard time from the lads. They'll take the piss out of me big time.'

Emma put the mirror down. 'It's when the guys are being nice to you that you need to worry.' She didn't seem to realize how embarrassing it all was. She was busying herself with bits of kit, ready to sort out my wound.

'Yeah. But really, you won't tell anyone, will you?' I was begging now, but it would be worth it if she would just agree to shut up about it.

'Please, Emma?'

She started cleaning the wound with some liquid and cotton wool. 'No, you're all right. I wouldn't be that cruel. Now, lie still and let me clean this thing up and close the wound. We don't want it getting septic, do we? Just think of the hard time you'd get then.'

As Emma cleaned and sewed, I gasped and winced with the pain, trying hard not to show how much it hurt. Then I noticed a big black rubber body bag lying in the corner of the tent. It had to be John. I'd heard that MERT hadn't been able to fly him out yet. No spare helis. They were still all up with D Company. I asked if I could take a look at him, but Emma shook her head. 'What for? You know what happened. You were there.'

She was right. I mumbled something about how dark and confusing it was out there, but to tell you the truth, I really had no idea

37

why I wanted to see him. What good would it do? Besides, Emma couldn't be persuaded. 'No, Briggsy. I haven't hosed him down yet. Remember him as he was. That's best.'

I nodded, but I wasn't sure if I agreed. Emma quickly changed the subject. 'Heard that one of them tried to take you last night . . .'

We were back on that old chestnut. Well, I wasn't going to tell the story again. It had been bad enough telling Si and the others the first time around. I just didn't want to think about it. But Emma kept on.

'I heard you shot him in the face. Sounds very frightening. And pretty full on for a guy who has only been here three weeks. You OK?'

I tried to shut her up fast. 'Yeah, it's what I get eighteen hundred quid a month for, isn't it?'

'Well, seeing as you're the new boy, and you've just had quite a major experience, and you can't run away because your combats are round your ankles . . . you are now going to get the potted Post Traumatic Stress Disorder lecture.'

I groaned loudly, but it wasn't like I had a choice. She banged on about all the symptoms of PTSD. Nightmares, mood swings, anxiety, that sort of stuff. Problems with alcohol and drugs. Trouble communicating with friends and family. Feelings of isolation, like nobody else understands. Violence. Even sexual problems.

We had watched a training film about it while I was at the Infantry Training Centre, but I'd fallen asleep halfway through. I'd been knackered after a day on the assault course. I wasn't really in the mood for hearing it all again, but then she said something I didn't know. She said PTSD normally took years to develop. Well that was news to me.

'So, Emma, you mean you might not even know you've got it until you're out the army and maybe even married with kids?'

'Exactly. And we need to remember that guys hit by PTSD are casualties of war, just like John. It's a normal reaction to an abnormal experience. There's even an American general with it.'

'Nah, you're joking.' I kept on looking down at the ground as she pressed on the wound.

'No joke. You heard of the Falklands war? It was years ago, early eighties?'

'Yeah, I have. I know a lot about it.'

'Bet you didn't know that since that war more guys have committed suicide as a result of PTSD than the 255 guys that were killed in action?'

'It's just a small percentage of people who develop PTSD. But if any of those symptoms start happening to you, you *must* get help.' Emma was looking at me like she expected me to be the very next sufferer.

'I'm not a jellyhead, I'm all right!' I

twisted round to look at her.

'I know, but it's my job to make sure you lot know.' She stood up and walked back over to her desk to put down her medical stuff. 'Right, you're done. You can get dressed. Seven days light duties and antibiotics.'

That wasn't what I wanted to hear. We might get sent back out and I'd be stuck in camp. I started to argue with Emma. 'But . . .'

'Don't care.' She pointed at me to shut up. 'Seven days light duties and I want you back here tonight after you've showered. Go easy—I want to check those sutures are still in place.'

By the tone of her voice, I could tell arguing with her wasn't going to get me anywhere, so I changed tack. 'You just want to see my arse again . . .'

'Your arse looks like a rancid badger's right now,' she giggled. 'Believe me, nobody's going to want to see it.'

I laughed back as I opened the tent flap to leave. Then the thought of walking back into the cookhouse stopped me. 'You're not going to tell anyone, are you?' I asked.

Emma looked me straight in the eye. 'I took the Hippocratic oath.'

I had no idea what that was but it sounded serious, which was good enough for me.

Chapter Six

As I walked over to the cookhouse, the familiar sound of generators humming and vehicles revving filled my ears. The Tannoy kicked off again, 'Standby. Standby. Firing. End of message.' Sure enough, another 70km Sniper kicked off and whooshed over my head. I couldn't be bothered to look up and watch it disappear into the sky without my sunglasses on. Besides, the most important thing on my mind just then was getting a brew.

Whenever we got any time off from being on patrol or on fatigues, it was always brew time. No doubt about it, the army would grind to a halt without tea. Even our ration packs had enough brew kit in them to supply all the Queen's garden parties put together.

The cookhouse was the centre of

our world. As well as having a brew on 24/7, we also got fed there, but more importantly it was where the telly was. BFBS, the British Forces Broadcasting Service, beamed in the soaps, news, music channels and, even better, football. There were always lads sitting in the cookhouse day or night. Just hanging around, chatting, watching telly, or reading all the three-week-old newspapers and magazines lying about.

The FOB was just a big square fort really, a bit like the US Cavalry outposts in the westerns I used to watch on Sunday afternoons. Only, instead of wood, they were made of Hescos. Hescos are massive, drum-shaped sandbags with a wire frame and they stood as tall as me. The engineers filled them with sand and stacked them up to make the FOB's perimeter walls, then they made buildings with them for protection against IDFs (indirect fire, rocket or mortar attacks). We didn't actually sleep in the Hesco buildings. We slept in tents surrounding them. We'd be too hot otherwise.

There was no air-conditioning and barely any plugs either. We used Solar Power Monkeys to keep our iPods and laptops charged up. It wasn't like there was a shortage of sun, if you know what I mean. I hadn't seen a single cloud since I'd been here. We were in the middle of the desert with nothing around us for miles. It was all generators, water wells and powdered milk. But you know what? It was great, I loved it. I even got thirty minutes of free phone calls home every week.

I pushed through the tent flap and into the cookhouse. Big mistake. About twenty lads all stopped chatting, farting and watching the telly, ready to take the piss out of me. There was a general chorus of 'Wey hey!' Then all the funnies started.

'It's the man with two arseholes!'

shouted Si with a big fat grin on his face.

'Not good, mate,' jeered Flash as he looked up from his magazine. 'Women ain't going to be impressed with that war wound.'

'*Guinness Book of Records* for you, mate,' shouted Jonesy without even looking away from the television. He was a lad from another platoon and he was a bit strange. No one understood his so-called joke, but then again we never understood what he was on about.

I felt the colour rise in my face as the piss-take continued. 'Nah, don't! Leave it out.'

Toki banged his chipped Best Dad in the World mug down on the bench and grinned up at me. 'Too late, mate. She was straight on the radio.'

Si, with half a jam sandwich stuck in his hand, plonked himself down on the bench beside Toki. 'Mate, s'pose you're going to be using twice as much bog paper now.' He obviously thought it was funny as he burst into a fit of hysterics.

I sat down opposite them both and resigned myself to hours of ritual torment. 'Yeah, yeah, yeah. Got any more?'

'Woah! Quiet, everyone.' Flash leapt over to the TV and turned the sound up. A blonde news presenter in a pink dress was going on about a famous singer being admitted to hospital for a suspected drug overdose. Apparently she had threatened to take legal action against some nightclub owner because his nightclub staff had let her get so drunk that she couldn't control her habit.

The news presenter than moved onto her second item of the day: 'Last night, another soldier was killed in southern Afghanistan. The latest British casualty died from wounds sustained during a clash with the Taliban . . .' After this very brief mention, the presenter went on to a story about their news team finding a talking dog in Southampton.

Si was not impressed. He strode up to the TV set, still munching on his sandwich, and turned the sound down. Spit and breadcrumbs fired out of his mouth as he shouted at the TV screen. 'That it? John's in bits and that's all he's worth? Shoved between a slapper and a dog? Don't they get what's going on out here!'

Flash looked unsurprised by the report or Si's outburst. 'Course not, mate. Come on, calm down and finish your sandwich.'

Si wasn't interested in finishing anything other than his rant. 'What do they think's happening? Patting kids on the head and giving out sweets? That all he's worth? Ten poxy seconds?'

Toki remained as calm as ever. 'What government would want people to know what's going on out here anyway?'

Si was about to respond with

another furious outburst when Flash butted in. 'They want them to see the sweets and the smiling Afghans. They don't want them to see us burying a lad's foot when we find it two days after his body has been sent back home. Not good PR, mate. I can understand that.'

Toki nodded at Flash. 'That's right. You've just got to get used to it, lads. Same as Basra. No one understands because they don't really know.'

'They don't want them to know,' added Flash as he pulled Si back to the table in front of his mug and the second half of his sandwich.

They both had a point. 'Yeah, MacKenzie got that about right this morning.' It was beginning to feel like MacKenzie was on the *Star Ship Enterprise* or something, because suddenly he materialized behind me.

'That's right, Briggsy, I always do.' He bent down and poked me in the chest. 'That's why it's Sergeant MacKenzie to you.'

49

'Yes, Sergeant,' I mumbled.

It seemed even Sergeant MacKenzie couldn't resist taking the piss: 'So, seeing as you are always talking out of your arse, are we all going to hear twice as much shit from you now?' He tipped back his head and roared with laughter at that one, and of course everyone else joined in.

I braced myself for more banter, but luckily MacKenzie had more important things on his mind. 'Shut up, everyone, and listen in. Warning Order. We are going back into the zone to finish the job. Orders at eighteen hundred, and no move before twenty hundred. All fatigue parties to have their jobs done before midday scoff so we have the afternoon to get prepped up. Let's go!'

'Sergeant . . .' I mumbled again. It was now or never. I didn't get a chance to get my sentence out, though. He already knew what I was going to say.

'No, Briggsy. Get yourself fit, then we'll get you back on the ground. Don't worry, we've still got another three months to go yet, mate. Now, get out there and burn those turd drums. We don't want yesterday's scoff floating about in them for too long, do we? Cookie might want to recycle.'

Chapter Seven

I hobbled over to the toilet block where Si and Flash were ready and waiting, armed with a couple of jerry cans of fuel. The bogs were pretty basic—just four fifty-gallon oil drums that had been cut in half for the Army to squat over. And once they were full of the FOB's shit and piss, it was our job to get rid of it all.

I lifted the cap off the jerry can I was holding and poured the fuel into the first drum. Flash did the same with the second.

Si watched us both as he giggled away to himself. 'You see the faces of those Yanks in here last week? When they saw we had oil drums to dump in, they couldn't believe it. Bet they get proper portaloos with, like, soft toilet paper and little Andrex puppies running around.'

He was probably right, but then

that meant they weren't getting extra pay to burn them out like we were. Thirty-five quid extra a week we got for volunteering for this job. Good stuff! I'd already managed to save up two and a half grand since joining the army, and the extra money was going to add to my savings.

My big plan was to buy a brand-new, black metallic Ford Focus ST. It was going to have the lot. Shiny badge on the front, eighteen-inch alloys, tinted windows, LEDs and the biggest woofer banging it out that Peckham had ever heard. I couldn't wait!

I wasn't the only one saving. Si was doing the same, although his purchase wasn't half as exciting as mine. Good. It was my chance to take the piss out of him for once. But I had to set him up for it first.

'Si, what colour's your new sofa gonna be?' I asked.

He beamed with pride. 'Red leather from DFS. Love it.' Si made it sound like he was buying a red BMW.

Flash slapped me around the back of the head.

'That's what happens when you get married. You sign up to a new boss; IKEA.' Flash spoke with the voice of someone who had been at it for years. 'Ain't that right, Si?' He was busy laughing as I rubbed the back of my nut.

'Yep. And I've got tons of kit to get. Sofa, leather chairs, and I wanna get a proper cot for the baby.'

I couldn't let that one go. I was in for the kill. 'See! Only nineteen and under the thumb already. What a sucker.'

Si leapt to defend himself as Flash gave me another slapping. 'Mate, I had to get married before coming out here, didn't I? Jakob's only six months old. What's gonna happen if I get zapped and we ain't married? Anna will go back to Poland and the boy won't even have my name. I had my mum's name because she never married my dad and that ain't happening this time.'

He had a point, so I decided to give up on the piss-take. Besides, Flash's slaps were getting harder every time. I signalled to the other two to stand back, then I took a box of matches out of my pocket. I struck one and threw it into the first stinking drum and we legged it fast. There was a big boom, then a whoosh as the flames roared into life and the turds began to burn.

Flash walked over to the second drum and took out his box of matches. 'You still got her picture inside your helmet, Si?'

'Yeah. And the boy's too.'

Flash chucked his match in and ran back to join us. We were still close enough to the heat and the stench of the burning drums for me to feel sick rise in my throat, but I swallowed it down. 'What you saving for, Flash?'

'Not saving, mate, surviving. I keep

telling you lads. There's a recession on out there. I'm here to help out my boys. Joe's getting married next year and Sam's got the world's biggest student loan. I'm definitely going regular after this. Get the kids sorted and get me and me missus a nice married quarter. Happy days.' It sounded like a good plan to me and I nodded my head in approval.

'You know what?' Flash gave a big grin. 'I don't mind being the oldest Rifleman on the planet and you lads giving me a hard time. It's ten times better than doing nothing back home, having to beg for money from the social. Getting made redundant has done me a favour.'

He jutted out his chin as if a heli was coming in to land on it. 'I like it here.'

I thought I'd had it bad being binned from the kebab shop in Peckham after only a week. They'd sacked me because I couldn't work the till properly. That's why I joined the army. Like Flash, I thought that's what you did when no one else wanted you. Mind you, it was beginning to sound like maybe I had it better than him.

'I like being here too.' I smiled back at him. 'It feels like something special.'

Flash nodded back at me. Talking with Flash was like having a big brother, something I didn't have back home. It was just me and Mum.

'You know, Flash, we're here doing something that no one I know back home will ever do. Know what I mean.'

We were obviously getting a bit too tree-huggy for Si. 'Oi, Richard and Judy, yous finished or what? Let's get on with it, there's still two more drums to do. It's nearly scoff time.'

Chapter Eight

I was standing in the cookhouse queue, starving as usual. No point asking Cookie what was for midday scoff. It was always the same two choices. Have it or leave it. Great sense of humour, old Cookie.

Mind you, there was one thing we definitely had better than the Americans and that was the food. We got ration packs to eat just like them, but the difference was, we had cooks to cook them up for us when we were in the FOB. Cookie worked wonders with a bag of powered egg and a tin of stewed beef. We also got fresh flown in from time to time. Stuff like spuds, bacon and fresh fruit. On the other hand, we didn't get fridges like the Yanks did. Most of the time you'd be seriously up for murdering your granny for a can of cold Coke.

Sergeant MacKenzie was hovering about like a vulture, shouting at each and every one of us to wash our hands before we ate. Brit soldiers must have the cleanest hands of all soldiers across the world. Vomiting and diarrhoea spread fast, and the whole company would go down if it wasn't controlled, so washing your hands was a really big deal.

Funny really, seeing as the rest of us was in rag order. Sweating so much our clothes stuck to our skin, and caked in dust like we'd gone ten rounds with a giant bottle of brown talcum powder—our hands were spotless though. We were made to wash them every chance we got, and always before eating or after having a dump. We got one shower a day for exactly three minutes. One minute soak, one minute soap, one minute rinse. But it was clean hands that mattered most.

The system seemed to be working

so far. The company hadn't had an outbreak of the squirts and shits since the lads got out there. Rumour said that the sergeants had a bet on between them about whose platoon was going to get the squirts first, and MacKenzie was definitely not going to be the one to lose that.

I held out my plate and Cookie slopped a ladle of mince and a splat of spuds on it, one beside the other, followed by a bit of green pond life around the edge of the plate. One of the things I loved about the army was the queuing system because I got to go to the front. Us riflemen got fed first, then NCOs like MacKenzie, and officers got fed last. When it came to food and kit, the lads always came first. At least there was one advantage to being low-life.

I picked up a knife and fork from the cutlery bin at the end of the counter. Everything was made of plastic—plates, cups, knives and forks—so everything could be chucked away in bin liners after every meal. It was cleaner that way, and would definitely go towards helping MacKenzie win that bet.

Just like the toilet waste, all used plastic was burnt too. Greenpeace would do their nut if they saw the black smoke that came out of our FOB. Mind you, if they wanted to worry about plastic, there was a lot worse for them to worry about in Afghanistan. The plastic high explosives the Talis used to make IEDs (Improvized Explosive Devices) did a serious amount of damage. The battalion had had more lads killed by IEDs than they ever had killed through getting zapped.

Cookie offered me spotted dick for afters, but I refused on the grounds that he said that to all the lads. He didn't bother to reply, just rolled his eyes skyward. He'd heard it all before, of course, but it was the law that you had to try and wind him up anyway, just for the fun of it.

I couldn't stop thinking about IEDs. Those things were just out there, buried in the ground, waiting for you to drive over them or step on them out in the field. Rumour also said that if you stepped on one, the last thing you'd hear would be a click as the connection was made between the electric charge and the detonator. I was more worried about IEDs than about getting zapped. I suppose it was because you had no control, no choice, you couldn't even fight back. It just happened or it didn't.

But it wasn't just Taliban IEDs that blew our soldiers up, it was the Russian mines too. They'd been buried in Afghanistan years ago, but they were still active. The Russian mines were called legacy mines, not that it mattered much to us who laid them or when. All that mattered to us was that there were thousands of them out there just a couple of inches under the ground and no one knew exactly where they were. Except, I suppose, some old Russian back in Moscow with the world's biggest map of Afghanistan stuck full of drawing pins.

Chapter Nine

I scraped my chair in next to Flash, who was using a spoon to get the mouthfuls in quicker. Si couldn't keep his eyes off the TV screen at the back of the room. Football repeats, of course, but he'd watch anything a hundred times over before even thinking about turning off the telly.

Flash stuffed a giant spoonful of meat into his mouth. 'Mmmm. Not bad. Not as good as me dad's mince, though. He makes the best.'

I picked up a fork and got stuck in too. 'Your dad cook, then?'

'Yeah. Better than me mum, even me missus. He does roast beef with big fat yorkshires every Sunday.'

Sounded good to me, but I couldn't really chip in with the Happy Childhood Memories game. 'Never saw my dad cook. Never saw him do anything really. He legged it before I started school.'

Flash always listened to what I had to say. 'Yeah? He was in the Falklands, wasn't he?' He barely got the words out before the spoon was loaded up and heading for his mouth again.

'Yeah. In the Guards.'

Si's eyes flicked away from the screen and he began pumping his arms up and down like he was marching. 'Oh the Guards . . . left, right, left, right, left, right . . .'

Flash lowered his spoon for a second and glared at Si before it was his turn to get a slap around the back of the head. 'Shut up, Si! Dickhead.' Si grinned and went back to his TV viewing. 'Go on, Briggsy, your dad was in the Guards?'

'Yeah, but I don't really remember anything about him, except that he was always drunk. Well, that's what my mum says. He used to come back home from the pub, give her a good slapping, and then disappear for days on end. My mum reckons the day she did a runner with me was the best day of her life. I don't think so, though, she still gets upset about it.'

Flash finished his meat and turned to his mashed potatoes. 'Harsh, mate. Harsh.'

Si looked away from the screen towards me. He'd obviously been listening as well as watching and eating. 'Poor little Briggsy,' he said in a sing-song voice, but his eyes didn't turn back to the telly.

I took a forkful of mince. 'Nah, it was all right. Mum got a job in the biscuit factory and we moved to a different estate. I got my own bedroom and everything, know what I mean?'

Flash was spooning so fast he'd got a big blob of mash stuck on his chin. He rubbed at it with the back of his hand, but the potato only spread out even more. 'Did your mum help you with your reading then, what with you having dyslexia and all that?'

'Nah. She didn't really notice. She was out working too much. She sort of feels guilty now, like it's her fault I'm in the army. The schools weren't any help. I didn't even know I was dyslexic until I joined up. I thought I was just thick! Well, I am . . .'

Flash started to rub his chin with two fingers in a more determined effort to get the spud off. 'You're not, mate.'

'I know, I know. Just a reading age of ten. Ain't good, though, is it?'

'How's the coursework going? Those educators squaring you away?'

'Yep. They've told me they're going to sort it. I've got loads of homework. Toki's still giving me a hand.'

'Good news. Listen, if you need any more help, give us a shout. Whatever you need.' Flash licked the mash off his fingers and was now moving on to the green stuff. Weird how he ate everything in separate portions, never mixing the different foods together.

'Thanks, but I'm doing all right. Know what? Joining up was the best thing I've ever done. Getting educated, being out here, doing the business.'

Someone scored a goal and the TV crowds roared. Si turned his attention back to the screen. He slapped his palm across his forehead, feeling the pain of the goal all over again, then he switched his focus back to us, his mates.

'If I hadn't joined up, I reckon I'd be in prison by now. That's where most of my old mates are. We were always getting into trouble. Just for stupid stuff, shoplifting, nicking cars, nothing serious. But then I started, like, getting pissed off with lads who had new cars, motorbikes, stuff like that. So I started to kick 'em in instead of nicking 'em. Smashed people's shops up just because they had stuff and I didn't. So I ended up in a detention centre down near Portsmouth when I was sixteen. Soft in the head, or what? Joining up was a good move, know what I mean?'

I nodded as Si started sipping his brew loudly. That was about the longest speech I'd ever heard Si make.

Flash nodded too. 'You know, the papers really get me ticking, the way they go on about hoodies and how all you kids are the scum of the earth. But you know what? They never write about teenagers like you two, or me boys. You lot have all bothered to get your finger out your arse and make a go of life.'

Si burst out laughing so much his brew came out of his nose. 'Briggsy's got two fingers out of his!'

Even I had to laugh at that one. We carried on eating in silence for a bit, and then Si started up again. 'You were lucky last night, Briggsy. Just think, what if that bullet had gone just a bit the other way? That would've been the end of your wedding tackle. Mate, what if it had gone any higher, it would have zapped your spine and you could be in a wheelchair for life. What if . . .'

I didn't really want to think about it, so I cut him off quick. 'Haven't really thought about it, mate.'

Flash pushed aside his empty plate and immediately reached for his bowl of spotted dick. 'Well, we're all pleased you're not dead, or being tortured by some drugged-up Tali right now.'

Si nodded and pointed his fork in my direction. 'Mate, you were lucky.'

I probably was, but it didn't mean I wanted to keep on going over and over it. 'Yeah, anyway.' I changed the subject. 'Anyone know why Toki joined up? If it really was to make his fortune, I reckon he messed up big time.'

Flash was now having trouble with the custard. It had missed his mouth by miles and was beginning to trickle down his chin in big yellow gobs. A little pool of it had even dripped down onto the table. 'Nah, probably just wants to fight, like all the Fijians. For him, it's recreation. He'll be in the army for the full whack. All the Fijians say they're staying in for life.'

Fortunately, someone shouted out that the welfare phones were back on, which meant I could get away from Flash and the yellow stuff. He'd somehow got it up his nose, so it looked like he had a big yellow bogey hanging out of one nostril.

'Got to go.' I scraped back my chair and stood up to leave.

'Going to phone that bird of yours again?' Si grinned and cupped his hands in front of his chest as if weighing two melons.

'Yeah, good one, Si. See ya!'

Chapter Ten

After queuing for about fifteen minutes, it was my turn to push aside the canvas curtain and enter the wooden stall. I picked up the receiver and dialled. Mum picked up the phone so quickly it was like she was hovering over it. She sounded relieved. 'Thank God you're OK. I've been watching the news all day, and when you didn't call I got so worried. You know what I'm like, thinking the worst and—'

'Mum, I keep telling you, I can't call when something happens. They cut the phones off until the family of the dead guy knows he's dead. Someone might phone the papers or whatever to try and make a few bob. The family needs to know first, don't they? But soon as they're working again, I call, don't I? Make sure you know I'm OK.'

She sighed so loudly I could hear it over the noise of some lads arguing about the football match as they stood in the queue.

'Yeah, you're a good boy. You're all right, and that's all that matters. I don't know what I'd do if anything happened to you. I sit and watch the news every day, smoking myself to death, just praying that—'

'Mum, I'm fine. Don't worry. I'm the new boy, they won't even let me out of the camp yet. Listen, I've been thinking about Dad and—'

I heard the sharp intake of breath and the change in her voice—a hint of anger mixed in with panic. 'What? He been writing to you? What does he want? Money? You tell him to keep away from us.'

I tried to sound calm, like it was nothing. 'No, he hasn't written, but...'

Her voice went up even higher. 'I ain't having him nowhere near us. He never lifted a finger to help us, why should we get involved with him now? What has he done to—'

I tried to talk over her. I just needed to get it out. 'But, Mum, I think he needs help. I think you should—'

It was hopeless. She was off again. 'Don't think, don't think anything about him. He's a drunk who never cared about us. Why should I worry about him? I have you to worry about.'

'Mum, I've been learning about PTSD. You know, combat stress. I think he might have it because of the Falklands stuff.'

It was no good. I had picked open an old wound and nothing could stop her now. 'Listen to me. I don't want to talk about him any more, and I don't want you even thinking about that man.'

'But Mum, just call him. Tell him to go see a doctor.'

'Why are you dragging all this up? What have I done to deserve this?

Haven't you given me enough to worry about? You calling just to get me even more upset? It's no fun back here you know. You think it's all . . .'

Then, as always, her anger quickly turned to guilt. 'I tried my best to bring you up good. I know I wasn't there all the time, but that's because that bastard didn't lift a finger to help us. I know I should have done more . . .'

I could hear the tears were about to come. Anything but that. I couldn't hack it when Mum cried. 'Mum, it's all right, you done good. I like the army. I'm sorry, forget it. Listen, I'll call in a couple of days because I've only got a couple of minutes left for this week on my phone card so—'

I cut myself off mid-sentence and put the receiver down gently. Stupid, stupid idea!

Chapter Eleven

I walked back to my tent and saw all John's stuff in bags and bin liners in one neat row on his bed. There was no sign of Flash and Si, but Toki was sitting on one of the plastic fold-up chairs with John's laptop resting on his knees. He must have carried on sorting through John's stuff during scoff. His fingers tapped and paused, tapped and paused on the laptop keys.

'He got any porn, Toki?'

Toki tapped again. 'Video of some contacts, a couple of pics of dead Taliban and some of Julie, just in stockings, that sort of stuff. Nothing terrible.'

The screen went black and he carefully closed the laptop. He pulled out the plug and started to coil the lead. 'I still hate doing this job, though.'

I nodded, though I wasn't really concentrating on what he was saying. I kept staring at the bed. All John's kit was in black plastic bags, while he lay in a big black rubber one. That was it when you died. That was all there was.

'I can't stay behind, Toki. I want to be out with you lot tonight.' The words came out thick and fast. 'Can't you talk with Sergeant MacKenzie . . . please?'

Toki looked up, his brown eyes showed concern. 'You OK?'

I tried to pull myself together. 'Yeah, I'm all right. Just don't want to be left behind when you lot go back out. The last thing I want is time on my own to think.'

Toki nodded at the plastic chair opposite him and I took a seat. 'You mean about last night, Briggsy?'

I took a deep breath. 'Yeah. Know what, the more I think about it, the more I think I just got lucky last night. I mean, what if I had got taken, or got a round in my spine. You know, the rest of my life in a wheelchair, like Si said. Feels worse than getting chopped up . . . I'm worried I might get out there next time and think too much about it and start flapping. Know what I mean?'

Toki looked down at my shirt and pointed at the brown stain. His voice was firm. 'Right, first thing, get that kit off and get washed and scrubbed. You don't need the smell of blood on you for a start.'

'It's not that, mate. It's, well . . . I'm more scared I'll let everyone down. I just want to get out there and not think too much about it.'

Toki sighed and nodded slowly, more to himself than to me. 'Sounds normal to me. All you have is self-doubt because it's all new and different, that's all.'

I suddenly felt pathetic, like a school kid again. 'I don't see any of you Fijian lads being scared of anything.' It came out more like a whine.

Toki paused for thought and then smiled. 'Everyone is, at some time or other. Anyone who says they have never been scared is either a liar, or has a screw loose in the head.'

I laughed at that, and Toki laughed with me. I was glad I'd come out with it. But Toki was lost in some memory of his own. He spoke slowly as if he was choosing his words very carefully. 'My first kill was in Basra. I was eighteen, too. We were on a strike op, hitting some houses right in the city centre. I got upstairs when a guy came out of nowhere with a knife—a big butcher's one. He jumped me before I could get my '80 up. We fell down the stairs fighting, I could smell his breath.'

Toki pulled his chair closer to mine and lowered his voice. 'I can remember his spit spraying in my face. He kept screaming as he tried to stab me with his knife. His eyes were really wide, like a mad man's. I had one hand trying to stop the knife going into my face, while I tried to get my bayonet out with the other.'

So Toki did know what it felt like. A thought crossed my mind. 'Why didn't you give him the good news with your pistol?'

Toki half closed his eyes and dropped his chin onto his chest, trying to get the bits of memory back in the correct order. 'We didn't all have pistols then. All I could do was keep head-butting him, but he wouldn't give up. I got my bayonet out and managed to stab him about four or five times in the neck. He died on top of me. I was soaked in his blood. Like you said, it was mostly down to luck. I started to worry that maybe I wouldn't be quite so lucky next time around, and that does your head in after a while. I kept worrying that I might let everyone down, or worse, end up getting one of my mates killed. You know, I still think of that Iraqi now and again, usually when I smell blood or cigarette breath. But you know how I get over that fear?' He leant his giant head forward so he was just an inch away from my face and looked me directly in the eye, waiting for me to ask.

'How?'

Toki's stare remained constant. Only his lips moved as he spoke, stressing every word as if each one was gold dust. 'I say to myself . . .' He leant into the back of his chair and raised himself to his full height for greater effect. 'I say to myself . . . Bollocks!'

I leaned back too, confused and disappointed. 'What? That it?'

Toki simply shrugged, raising his hands towards the roof of the tent before letting them fall down at his sides again. 'That's all you need. Look, I'm a soldier, right? And as the saying goes, "You choose your branch, you take your chance." It's not for everyone, but everyone doesn't have to be here, do they?'

I shook my head, but I wasn't really sure I was getting any of this. 'No, suppose not. So?'

'And so, bollocks to it.' Toki looked triumphant, as though he had discovered the mystery of the universe. Then he spoke almost in a whisper, as though he was sharing the biggest secret of them all.

'When I'm out there and it's all kicking off, I reckon I'm probably dead anyway. So anything I do to stop that from happening to me or my mates is a bonus. Do you get it?' He looked towards me eagerly, with a big smile on his face.

It felt like I was talking to some Jedi master out of *Star Wars*, but I still didn't get it. 'S'pose so,' I said, more to please him than anything else.

He looked a bit disappointed by his Jedi trainee's lack of enthusiasm, so he added a final explanation. 'Listen, I know you won't lose your nerve because you want to stay alive. You've proved that. Plus, you know you've got an even bigger responsibility to keep your mates alive, and I know you would never let them down, would you?'

I hung on to every word, hoping that in the end it would all make sense to me. 'Hope not.' I know I still sounded a bit reluctant, but it was the best I could manage. I gave him a weak smile to show that I really appreciated the effort he was making.

'Listen, you'll be all right.' He smiled back, like he knew it was time to lighten the mood. 'You haven't sent a bluey to your mum this week, so let's see how your writing's improved. Then we'll do a bit of that coursework. Maybe then I'll think about talking to Sergeant MacKenzie for you.'

That was the best news I'd had

since our chat began. The rest I needed to think about. Now that we were back on safer territory, I had a sudden brainwave. 'You know what? I think I'll write to my dad instead. It'll be the first time. There's something important he needs to know about. There are gonna be a few words I learnt about today that I can't spell . . .'

I reached for a bluey from the neat stash of them under Si's bed, and fumbled for the pen in the bottom of my pocket. I began to write, stopping every so often for Toki to check and help me with my spelling.

Dear Dad,
Hope you are OK. I don't know your postcode but reckon this should get to you OK. Because me and Mum haven't seen you for years, you probably don't know that I'm in the Army now. Well, the bluey gives it away I suppose!

I'm in Afghanistan and I've got about three months left. I'm in the Rifles as it happens, not the Guards. Mum's OK. She just worries a lot. Anyway, Mum told me that when you were in the Falklands, you were on a ship attacked by Argie planes. She said the ship got blown up and lots of your mates got burnt really bad, and some of them died. Maybe why everything went pear-shaped between you and Mum afterwards is because you have Post Traumatic Stress Disorder.

Dad, PTSD is something that loads of soldiers get, but the doctors can help you. Just go and see one. Please . . .

The FOB's loud speaker system sparked up again. 'Standby. Standby. Showers are on, but today, only for an hour. The pumps need a service.

End of message.'

Toki picked up John's laptop. 'Leave the letter, Briggsy. We'll finish it off later. Go clean yourself up.'

Chapter Twelve

After showering and changing my shirt as Toki had instructed, I wandered back over to the Medic Centre. Emma still had the Chili Peppers banging out of her speakers when I finally got called in. It was a wonder she was able to concentrate on any kind of medical emergency with those twats warbling in the background. I was more of a Jay–Z man myself.

'Emma! I'm back.'

I was still pissed off with her for telling the lads about my war wound. She might be pretty, but she was definitely a pain in the arse. And I had one of them already!

I decided to go straight into attack mode. 'I can't believe you told 'em.'

She looked puzzled for a moment, as though she wasn't quite sure what I was talking about. 'Hmmm . . . Did

I? . . . I can't remember . . .'

She squirted her hands with disinfectant from a bottle and burst into fits of laughter. 'That's what you get for having a go at my music.'

I smiled like I thought it was all a fantastic joke, but I wasn't letting her get away with it that easily. 'That was bad. What about your Hippy oath thing?'

She laughed again. 'I haven't taken an oath, you dickhead. I'm a medic, not a doctor. Besides, you can't blame me. It was just too good to keep to myself.'

I undid my combats and lay on the bench again, carefully pulling my underpants down along with my trousers, so as not to disturb the wound that was trying hard to scab up. I turned my head to one side to watch her as she came over.

'I *do* blame you. I've been ripped apart all day.'

She showed no pity, though. 'Well, tough. The deed is done. Now, let's have a quick look. How has it been?'

'Fine now, thanks. I reckon it's better.' Then I ruined it by flinching big time as she ripped off the dressing and started prodding me.

'Yeah, right.' She wasn't fooled by my speedy recovery act. 'I can tell it's still painful, but at least there's no weeping. Looks like it's healing well. I'll just give it another quick clean.'

I hoped she was feeling a bit guilty about telling the others, so I made my move. I twisted my head round further to try and make eye contact. 'Can you tell Sergeant MacKenzie I'm good to go, then? It would make up for making me look like a right idiot.'

'Your trouble is, you have no sense of humour.' So far, so good, at least I'd got a smile out of her.

'Yeah, that's right. It's a laugh a minute being known as the man who needs two lots of bog paper.' I looked back down at the plastic floorboards again.

Emma didn't respond. She was too busy doing her cleaning and swabbing stuff. It hurt like hell, but I tried to talk through the pain.

'Talk to Sergeant MacKenzie for me? Please, Emma.'

'We'll see . . . There. You're done.' And with that, she walked back to the desk and started to write up some medical notes. As I got dressed, I couldn't help but stare at the big black body bag again.

'John.' I hadn't realized I had said his name out loud until she answered.

'What about him?'

I didn't even know why I was asking. 'Can I see him? You must have cleaned him up by now.'

Emma's voice was softer, kinder. 'You sure that's what you want?'

I gave a nod. 'Yeah. Quick goodbye before he goes.'

Emma put down her pen and turned off the Chili Peppers. There was a long zip noise as she slowly opened the body bag so just his face was showing. She didn't want me to see the wounds. We both stared at John for a while without speaking. It looked almost like he was sleeping, but his face looked weird. His skin was grey, not sunburnt like it was yesterday. It was Emma who broke the silence. She sounded like she was trying to put a brave face on it.

'Don't worry, he will look a lot cleaner by the time his family gets to see him. They'll put make-up on him and wash his hair. He should get to Kandahar tonight. He'll be back home soon.'

I couldn't find any words. 'Uh-huh,' is all that came out. There was another long pause before Emma spoke again. Her voice was small and less sure than usual. 'First body you've seen?'

'Well, first one of us. Talis don't count, do they?'

'Not good, is it? You all right?'

I swallowed hard. 'Yeah. He

doesn't really look like John any more with that skin, does he? Know what I mean?'

She asked me again. 'Sure you're OK?' I could only nod in response.

'Well, I'm not,' she sounded upset as she zipped up the body bag. 'I don't think I can go on looking at dead soldiers much longer.'

That surprised me as I would have thought she'd be used to it. Now there was no holding her back.

'I am TA and this is my third and final tour, Briggsy.' Her voice wavered slightly as she spoke.

'You getting some of those stress symptoms you told me about, then?'

'No. Course not. I'm a paramedic back home. I've seen more blood and guts than you ever will. But you know what? This is different.'

I looked her in the eye and waited to find out why.

'Because I know John. I've known all of them. I know each and every guy stuffed in one of those body bags, and each and every guy who arrives here with an arm or leg blown off. I live with you, eat scoff with you, have a laugh with you, even use the same drums to dump in as you, but you know what?' A tear started to roll down her face and she brushed it away angrily. 'Bring on Glasgow's house fires, car crashes and Saturday night stabbings. If I can't save them, then at least I don't have to be mates with them.'

A helicopter flew over our heads and interrupted her outburst. We both looked up towards the sky, as if we could see through the canvas above us. 'That'll be for John.' Emma went back into medical mode again. 'The rest will be here soon to get you lot back out on the ground.'

The sound of the heli got louder as I opened the tentflap. I couldn't get out of there fast enough. I turned just before I made my exit, 'Talk to Sergeant MacKenzie, Emma. Please.'

Chapter Thirteen

I went back to the tent and Toki helped me finish the bluey to my dad before evening scoff. There wasn't so much piss-taking now as everyone had the Green Zone on their minds, including me. MacKenzie had given Toki the go-ahead. I was going back out to the Green Zone with the rest of the lads that night.

After scoff, I spent quarter of an hour queuing for the phone. I thought I'd better call Mum again. She'd only get herself in a state otherwise. She sounded OK as soon as she realized it was me. She sounded like the happy, smiling mum off the Oxo adverts, but I wasn't falling for it that easily.

'Mum. Listen, sorry about the call earlier.'

'That's all right.' She was so cheery, she sounded like she was offering me a KitKat. 'I know I get a bit worked up sometimes, David. You know, being on my own and all that.'

I think she was hoping we could leave it there, but I needed to get through to her once and for all. 'Look, Mum, I think we have to have a straight-up talk. I don't blame you for me being in the army. I chose to be here. It's what I want. I like being a soldier. Nobody made me join the army, and the day I don't like it any more, I'll get out. I'm a man now, Mum, I'm proud of myself. You've done a brilliant job. You know that, don't you?'

I heard her sniff then, trying to fight back the tears. Her voice quivered as she spoke. 'I tried so hard. It's just that it felt like you left me cos I didn't do enough for you when you were younger. I wanted to be there but . . .'

She had it all wrong, as usual. It was nothing to do with that. 'Mum, it's OK, I know. You should be proud of what you have done for me. I am. Listen, everything is good. We're OK, yeah?'

She gave another big sniff and started to recover a little. 'Yeah, course we are.' She gave a little laugh to prove it. I kept going with what I wanted to say. 'That's good, because I got to tell you stuff . . . I've sent a letter to Dad.'

'Oh, David . . .' The crying immediately started again.

'Mum, if you can't help him, I've got to. He needs help, Mum. That's why I wrote to him, Mum. You understand?'

Her crying was getting louder now.

'Mum, you OK?'

She pulled herself together then and put her cheery Oxo mum voice back on. 'Yeah, I'm all right. You've always been a good boy. I just miss you. It's not easy being on my own. Sometimes I even miss your dad. Even when he was being a bastard, at least he was here.' She laughed at her own bad joke.

'I know you miss him, Mum. I know.'

She was off down memory lane again now. I'd heard it all before, but funnily enough, I quite liked her going on about how things used to be. Made us sound like a proper family for once. 'We used to love dancing. Disco mad, your dad and I were. He was a right John Travolta.' We both laughed at the image of Dad doing a bit of *Saturday Night Fever* on the dance floor.

'Bet both of you looked a nightmare in flares and platforms, Mum.'

'We looked fantastic!'

Just then the phone beeps started to go. I spoke in a rush to get the words out in time. 'Mum, card's gonna run out soon. I can't call for the next four or five days, so don't worry or . . .'

'What's happening? You doing anything dangerous?' The worry was

97

back in her voice again.

'Mum, it's all right. I just have to wait for my new phone card, that's all.'

'I love you.'

'Me too, Mum.' Then the phone line went dead.

As I put down the phone, I suddenly felt very alone. I missed my mum, even though I really did want to be out in Afghanistan. I felt my eyes prickle with tears and decided to stay where I was for a bit to calm down. Didn't want the lads to see me blubbing, did I? They would have even more to take the piss out of. I sniffed loudly, trying to fight back the tears, and hoped that no one could hear me on the other side of the canvas.

I'd been telling everyone I wanted to get back in the Green Zone, but now that I'd got it, I wasn't sure if I wanted to go after all. It just didn't feel exciting any more. To be honest, I wasn't sure I could hack it. It was just luck that I'd got myself out of a drama and killed that Tali. What if I couldn't do it again? Si had really got me thinking and I was pretty scared now. I was hoping Toki was right about me. But what if I ended up letting my mates down when it mattered most?

I quickly wiped my eyes before pulling aside the canvas flap. I had to switch on and get a grip of myself before we started shooting the Taliban once again.

Chapter Fourteen

It was about five-thirty in the morning and we had been back out in the Green Zone for over seven hours. It wasn't going well. We had been in major contacts with the Taliban all night long and, in the confusion, lots of us had got split up from our platoons.

MacKenzie had ordered our four-man patrol to move to a new location so he could link up with us, but that was easier said than done. Firstly, it was pitch dark so we couldn't see where we were going. Secondly, during all the fighting, we'd got surrounded by Taliban. They were taking regular pot-shots at us, and judging by the amount of fire coming our way, we were seriously outnumbered.

Toki got on the radio to MacKenzie to let him know that we

couldn't move anywhere. Worse still, our ammunition was seriously low. We had completely run out of ammo for our rifles, and we'd only got about half a mag left on our pistols, so we had about six rounds each left. That was it.

MacKenzie said he would send two Apaches out to us. They'd be there in thirty minutes. Once they started firing their 30mm cannons into the maize fields, we'd have plenty of fire cover to get out. All we had to do was stand our ground until they arrived. Toki said MacKenzie had wished us all luck. The Tali rounds were getting closer by the minute, so it looked like we were going to need it.

I wiped the sweat off my mud-caked face, and tried taking deep breaths to calm my breathing. It wasn't working. 'Toki, they're getting closer, mate.'

'We are all right, Briggsy. They're just firing into the dark, trying to flush us out.'

'They will soon. It's nearly first light.' I was beginning to wonder if we were going to get out of this one. Another twenty minutes or so and the sun would be up—and there was no way we weren't going to be seen.

Flash was obviously thinking the same thing, and when he spoke, I could hear that he too was breathing heavily, which made me feel a lot better. 'How we going to stand our ground until the Apaches get here?'

'Mate, soon as it's light, they'll be able to see us,' added Si. He sounded as scared as the rest of us. 'Mate, we've got no ammo.'

We fell silent for a moment, and waited for Toki to come up with something. I was desperate for him to come up with anything that sounded like a plan.

Just then, two of the Taliban started shouting at each other in between firing off a few rounds across the maize. They definitely had a plan, and chances were it involved us.

My heart was beating even faster by the time Toki finally spoke. 'OK, listen in.'

We all moved an inch closer to him so as not to miss a word. 'Soon as it becomes light enough for us to see where we are going, we move to the edge of the maize and take cover in the irrigation ditch that runs in the open ground. That way we can wait up until the Apaches start hosing down the fields, plus we don't need to worry about getting hit by their rounds. Then, once they've done their bit, we can start moving and link up with Sergeant MacKenzie. Any questions?'

I had one. 'I've only got four rounds left—that's it. What happens if we run into them on the way out?'

There was a short pause before I heard the sound of grating metal. 'Fix bayonets,' came the reply.

I didn't keep mine in its metal

sheaf like Toki, so I pulled my bayonet out from where I had jammed it into the webbing of my body armour. I twisted it into the barrel of my rifle, and checked and double-checked it was on tight.

This was getting really scary. I'd never actually used one before, at least not in real life. I'd only done it back in the UK while we were training. We'd practised screaming at sand bags as we charged towards them making what was supposed to be a terrifying face. You had to put on a war face to frighten the enemy as well as rev yourself up a bit. That way you'd be able to do the business with your bayonet when you finally reached him. It was all a bit of a laugh in training. I never really thought I might have to do it for real.

Si was feeling the pressure, too. 'Mate, we're outnumbered. There are shedloads of 'em out there.'

Toki's voice remained calm as ever. 'If we move through the maize slowly and quietly, we shouldn't bump into any of them. But if it kicks off, we'll take them one at a time. That's right, isn't it, Briggsy?'

I managed to mumble a yes, but it didn't sound very convincing.

Toki ignored my fear and carried on. 'In here, they're going to have to be within a metre or so before they see you. And when they do, you got to be quick. Remember, grip the weapon. Get your body behind it, the butt tucked in under your arm. Ram that lump of metal into him before he has a chance to do anything to you. Aim for the centre of what you can see of him. His bones and kit will resist a little, so keep your body weight behind the weapon. Take him down, leave him dead or alive, and just keep moving on. Fight your way out of the field and take cover in the ditch.'

Flash spoke quietly but urgently. 'It's first light, Toki.' He was right. The eight-foot-high maize field was beginning to take shape.

'You ready?' Toki fixed his eyes on Flash, who took a gulp of air before he answered slowly and steadily, 'Ready.'

Toki then checked out Si, although to be honest, when his reply came he sounded less sure.

Toki then fixed his eyes on me. 'You ready?'

My mouth was so dry I couldn't get the words out.

'Briggsy, you ready?' he repeated.

I swallowed hard and tried to sound confident. 'Ready.' It was more of a squeak than an answer.

Toki started to move through the maize, 'Single file, behind me.'

Chapter Fifteen

Flash and Si fell in and I followed behind, each of us a couple of metres behind the other. We needed to be spread apart as much as possible to prevent a burst of Tali fire taking all four of us down at once, but not so far apart that we couldn't see the next man in front.

The maize rustled as we pushed ourselves through. I held the pistol-grip of my rifle with my right hand. My left was around the barrel, keeping the bayonet raised, ready to take on anyone who came near. I desperately hoped they wouldn't. With just a few rounds each, staying hidden was going to be our greatest weapon.

As I inched my way slowly through the field, a head of corn banged against my shoulder and made me jump like a startled rabbit. Even a snap of straw under my feet made me flinch. I could still only see about two metres ahead of me, but I could hear all four of us breathing heavily.

Every so often the Taliban would let out one of their bloodcurdling screams and a whole load of them would open fire with their AK47s. We would duck down automatically every time it happened, praying that the rounds weren't heading our way. Toki kept us moving forward as quickly as we could.

All of a sudden, Si screamed out, 'Contact right! Contact right!' All four of us turned. I could just make out the shape of two men as one of them fired wildly in our general direction. We all fired a few puny rounds into the thick maize as they zipped past us then quickly disappeared.

'Out of ammo! RV. Get to the RV!' shouted Toki and we broke into a run. I was still last in line, huffing and puffing, sweating in my body armour and helmet, terrified I might get left behind.

There was a burst of fire from the Taliban to my right, then an ear-piercing scream stopped me in my tracks. It came from one of us.

'Man down! Man down!' I crashed through the maize to try to reach whichever one of us had been hit, but I still couldn't see through the thickness. Toki's voice hit me from about five metres ahead. 'Keep moving! He's dead. Go, go!'

More fire came from my right as I carried on running, jumping over Flash's body on the way. He was face down, soaked in blood. More fire followed from the left, and then from behind. I still couldn't see anything except maize. Another round of fire burst out from ahead of us. I started to panic. 'Toki!'

Before I could decide which way to run, Si was screaming at me. 'Briggsy! Left. Tali, left! Look left!'

There was a Taliban just a metre to

my left. Dark eyes wide open, teeth bared, his beard glistening with sweat. There was nowhere to run.

I don't know who screamed the louder, but both of us yelled at the top our lungs as we hurled ourselves towards each other. I gripped my weapon and lunged as hard as I could. The bayonet made contact with his chest. His dark eyes took one last look down the barrel of my weapon as his shirt and skin resisted for a second before giving way under the bayonet's blade. I heard a squelch as the cold, hard steel resisted a little against bone.

I pushed in harder, my war face now just inches from his as we both screamed at each other. The bayonet forced its way past his ribs and rammed all the way home into his chest. He gave one long scream as his knees buckled and he fell backwards, pulling me forward with him. There was no way I was going to let go of my rifle.

It was then that I realized my bayonet was stuck in his chest. My rifle was practically standing upright all on its own now that the Tali was down on the ground.

'What you doing? Leave him! Come on!' Si's voice hovered between exhaustion and panic.

'I can't get it out. It's stuck in his ribs!' Si took hold of my rifle's grip, putting his hands on top of mine.

'Pull, Briggsy, pull!'

We pulled together, wiggling and twisting to pull the blade free. There was another squelch and a rasping noise as the bayonet slid out stiffly from between two ribs. I stood stock still, watching the blood drip slowly down the blade.

Si's voice cut through my daze. 'Run, Briggsy, run!' More rounds came from all directions. I scanned every shape ahead of me but still couldn't see him. 'Where's Toki?'

'Keep going!' Si was panting so heavily he could hardly speak. 'Do as he said, the RV!'

I increased my speed to catch up with Si and we ran the last ten metres together to the edge of the field. In the distance, I could hear the two Apache attack helicopters approaching. I scanned the horizon but couldn't see them. It didn't matter.

They would arrive soon and sort this drama out good style. I scrambled quickly into the cover of the ditch, and slid down the mud until I was up to my knees in cold water.

Chapter Sixteen

The two of us crouched in the ditch, our helmets sticking up over the top just enough for us to make sure no Talis were following. Not that we could have shot them anyway.

Si was right next to me, still panting after the run. 'Mate,' he whispered in between gulps of air. I turned my head. The sweat dripping down his face was turning the streaks of mud to a wet paste. He gave me a big grin, his jagged white teeth flashing against his shiny skin.

'Happy days or what, we made it!'

I grinned and nodded, but to be honest I didn't feel the same relief. I could only focus on one thing. 'Where's Toki?' We looked back at the field, scanning every inch of maize.

'Look!' Si's arm shot out as he pointed. 'Edge of the maize. Half left.'

Sure enough, there was Toki, bent forward with Flash's body draped around his shoulders. I jumped and waved my arms in the ditch.

'Toki, quick. Over here!' As he looked up to hear where my voice was coming from, he hitched Flash further up his shoulders and headed towards us.

'Woah!' Si gripped his weapon tightly but remained stock still. 'Talis!'

Four Taliban had sprung out of the maize. They didn't appear to be taking aim with their AKs, but were running straight for Toki, and they were catching up with him fast.

Like Si, I too was frozen to the spot. Couldn't speak, couldn't move, could only look on in terror. Si's voice came through in short, sharp, terrified bursts. 'Mate, what do we do? What do we do?'

As the Taliban closed in on Toki and Flash, they began to scream out.

It sounded like Indians attacking a wagon train in one of those old black and white westerns. Toki dropped Flash to the ground and looked wildly about him. He swung his weapon up, ready to fight, his bayonet glinting in the early morning sun. 'Come on, you bastards! Come on!' he screamed back at them. He had worked out what was happening before we did.

I felt Si grip my shoulder. 'They're not shooting . . .'

My eyes didn't leave Toki as he stood over Flash. A wave of panic spread through me. 'That's because they're trying to take him!'

As I watched Toki stand his ground waiting for the Talis to come to him, something shifted within me. It began to rip through my heart and churn my guts, twisting and turning inside. Without thinking, I began to scramble up the bank.

'Where you going?' Si already knew the answer.

115

'Come on!' It didn't matter whether he was going to follow or not.

'Mate, we only got bayonets.' Si's voice was pleading, but he was already scrambling up the bank to join me.

I looked across the hundred metres of open ground at Toki, preparing to fight to the death, and a wave of emotion blasted through my body. It seared through my lungs, roared through my throat and finally broke free. 'Bollocks!' I screamed and broke into a run.

I kept my focus on Toki as I raced across the field. He stabbed his bayonet at the first Taliban, who dropped to his knees, wounded in the shoulder. But the other three were too quick. They kicked and punched Toki to the ground, took hold of his arms and legs, and started to bundle him back towards the maize. As they dragged him off, Toki writhed and screamed until the tallest one hit him over and over again with the butt of his rifle. The tall one then ran back to help his injured friend, who'd got hold of Flash by one of his heels. Flash didn't resist as they dragged him off in the same direction as Toki. He couldn't. But he lifted one arm to protect his head as it banged against the rocks jutting out of the ploughed field. He was still alive!

As I ran towards my mates, it was as if my head knew what my body wanted to do and it just sort of happened. All sound became muffled. I was sure Si was following me, but I couldn't actually hear him. I knew I was screaming out loud, but I could barely hear any sound come from my mouth. The Apaches must have been approaching, but I wasn't aware of the roar of their rotor blades. I was running in slow motion and all that mattered was getting Flash and Toki back, nothing else. I had to get amongst it. I had to help them. I couldn't have stopped myself even if I'd wanted to. I just kept on running, kept focusing on Toki and Flash getting dragged closer and closer to the maize, where they would be lost to me for ever.

This time my war face just happened. I didn't have to think about it, but I knew it was there. I wasn't scared of the Taliban or frightened of dying. There were more important things to think about: my mates.

I took the final few bounds towards them and crashed into the tall Tali who was dragging Flash. My bayonet slid into the side of his chest like butter. It must have helped that I was running at full speed when I smashed into him. I didn't even slow down to take aim. The Tali fell backwards slowly, screaming. Or at least he looked like he was screaming as he had his mouth wide open.

Out of the corner of my eye, I was

aware that Si was taking on the wounded Tali, but I kept on looking at Toki. He was being dragged by his arms by the other two and they had just reached the gap in the maize.

I set my sights on the one nearest me. With my rifle gripped firmly, just like Toki said, I aimed for centre mass and charged. Concentrating on my target, I was barely aware that I was screaming my head off.

Everything happened slowly and clearly. I saw both Talis look up at me as I got closer. They dropped Toki's arms and started grabbing their AKs from their slings. It didn't bother me. I knew I was going to be faster. I jumped over Toki's blood-stained face and landed on top of my man. My bayonet plunged into the right-hand side of his neck and he dropped at my feet. With his windpipe shredded, he was slowly suffocating.

I turned to the next, but he had already bottled it and vanished into the maize. I didn't bother to follow. Behind me, Si was checking out Flash, the injured Tali lying dead by his side.

As if on cue, the two Apaches started shooting the maize field. Every few seconds, the whirr of rotor blades was broken up by the rattle of cannons as their thermal sights found what they were looking for. The ejected 30mm cases rained out from underneath the helis, one of them bounced off my helmet with a metallic thud.

Chapter Seventeen

As the Apaches did the business in the maize fields, Si and me got Toki up and limping, then we dragged Flash halfway down the ditch.

As soon as we were in cover, Toki got straight on the radio to MacKenzie to give him our exact location and to report on the state of our casualty. The blood on Toki's face had already dried in the sun and there was a nasty cut on his lip. He was definitely going to be battered and bruised for a good few weeks to come, but at least there was no major damage done.

Flash was another story. We'd managed to stretch him out on a slight shelf just above the waterline. Si and me had cut off his combats, and just about stopped the bleeding in his leg, but he had a big, fat hole ripped out of the middle of his thigh.

Si had pumped him full of morphine, but it didn't sound like it was working that well. He wasn't screaming, but he wasn't exactly talking much either. We stayed close, even though there wasn't much more we could do. We just tried to chat to him a bit, so at least he knew his mates were with him as we waited for MERT to arrive.

Flash's face screwed up in pain. 'I can't feel my leg.'

'You're alive, mate, that's all that matters.' I really meant it.

Toki came off the radio. 'MacKenzie says just two more minutes and MERT will be here to lift us all out.'

I felt a surge of happiness rush through me. 'Hear that, Flash. MERT will be here in two. You got us going back there, you know. Thought you were a gonner.'

'So did I.' He managed to grimace. 'I blacked out when I got zapped. Next thing I knew, Toki was there.'

'Just making sure you were properly dead,' Toki smiled and his lip bled some more. Si and me burst out laughing like it was the funniest thing we'd ever heard. I don't know why. It wasn't much of a joke. I looked around at all three of them, brimming with happiness. 'We made it! We all made it!' I pumped my arm in the air. '*Yessssss.*'

Si beamed back at me. 'Happy days!'

Just then, the faint sound of the MERT Chinook filled the air. I looked up to find the dot in the sky but couldn't see it yet. It didn't matter, it would be here soon.

I put my hand on Flash's arm. 'Hey, Flash, the doctors are nearly here, mate. You'll be in hospital with that gammy leg of yours within the hour.'

'Briggsy!' Toki barely took his eyes off the sky as he threw me a smoke grenade. 'Mark us up so the heli doesn't land on top of us. Give it some blue a good twenty metres from the ditch. You know what those RAF are like.'

I leapt to my feet like I'd just been asked to pick up my winnings on the lottery. 'Okey-dokey, Toki!' I giggled as I caught the baked-bean-can-sized grenade.

Funny how things turn around. You think you haven't got it in you, then you find out you have. When the Tali started dragging Toki and Flash back into in the maize, it was my time to prove I had what it took. I did my job, good style. Si did too. For me, that was a big relief.

Even bigger was that I was still alive to think about it. I didn't feel good or bad about killing. It was just them or me really. But I know one thing for sure, back there by the maize was the first time I felt like a real soldier.

I scrambled up the bank and ran into the open ground. I could now see the Chinook clearly, about six or seven hundred metres away. I pulled the pin, threw the grenade and a thick cloud of blue smoke filled the air. The Chinook slowly turned and headed towards us. Happy, happy days!

Under the cover of smoke, Toki climbed up the bank to meet me. He cupped his hands to his mouth to shout above the sound of the rotor blades.

'Hey, Briggsy! I was right, wasn't I? You did good back there.'

I grinned as I walked towards him, enjoying the praise. 'Looking at the way you were mincing about with those Talis,' I shouted from about two metres away, 'I thought you could do with the help. Besides, I had to help my mates out, didn't I? Happy d—'

I heard a click underneath my foot. Nothing else.

Chapter Eighteen

Two months later and I was back at home in my old bed. My room hadn't changed since before I'd joined the army. It still had Chelsea posters stuck all over the walls, and my old skateboard propped up behind the door.

The only thing different was that Mum had Blu-Tacked a couple of army photos next to my poster of Beyoncé. There was one of me and the lads on the assault course at the Infantry Training Centre, and a big group shot of the whole platoon, who were still back at the FOB with another month left to go of the tour. Si had sent me that one while I was still in hospital. His arse was in the middle of the picture doing a moonie, with all the others grinning behind him, giving me the thumbs up.

Apparently, when I had trodden on the mine, there was just a small explosion and some dirt got thrown up into the air. You kind of expected a fire and a blast of epic proportions if it was going to change your life that much, but it hadn't happened that way. The explosion hadn't thrown my body high into the air. It had just sort of lifted me off the ground about six inches. Trouble was, when I landed, I was no longer in one piece, but two. I lost most of my right leg in the blast.

It was Toki who hadn't stood a chance. The force of the explosion had hurled lumps of rock straight towards him at supersonic speed. A shard of rock had flown up into his chin and sliced straight through his brain. He was killed outright.

At least Flash was doing well. He had called me yesterday from his new married quarters. His missus loved it. He had a massive scar on his leg and was still in a lot of pain, but he would be fit enough to stay in the army. Good news.

Si emailed me all the time. The lads back at our FOB were still getting shot at by the Talis most nights. Other than that, he was busy burning turd drums for his red leather sofa. He told me that after Toki was killed, MacKenzie had given him a really good send-off.

It felt strange not being out in Afghanistan with the lads any more. Some days I felt guilty for surviving when Toki hadn't. But on other days, when the pain in my leg was really bad, I reckoned maybe Toki had the better deal.

I tried not to think too much about what life would be like in the future. Better just to crack on with it. Wait and see, know what I mean? The doctors said once my leg had healed well enough, they'd be able to fit a false one to the stump.

Having to leave the army was the worst thing really, but I still planned to keep in touch with all my mates. And like MacKenzie said in all his speeches, I would make sure I never forgot Toki, or any of the lads killed in action wherever they fought.

People like Toki lived and died as soldiers, doing a job they loved. For some reason, back in the UK, no one seems able to get their heads around that fact.

Soldiers don't fight for Queen or country, like they say on the telly. They fight for each other. It's the job of a soldier to kill the enemy, and if that means getting killed or injured in the process, so what? Toki and all the rest of them who died knew the risks. Toki wouldn't want any pity. And if he didn't want any, then I didn't either.

One good thing that had come out of all this was that I was starting to get my dad back. The second half of that letter I'd posted to him from Afghanistan said he could write back to me if he wanted. I'd told him I'd post him some pictures of me in my uniform, and maybe he could send some of him from when he was in the Army.

Things moved on quite a bit after that. My dad went to see a doctor about PTSD and they started giving him some help. He even came to see me in hospital last week, and drove me and my mum back home just now. Maybe they'd get back together one day. Who knew?

One thing I did know, though, was once a soldier, always a soldier. Know what I mean?